KINGFISHER READERS

level 3

Cars

D0172669

Chris Oxlade and
Thea Feldman

KINGFISHER
NEW YORK

KINGFISHER
LONDON & NEW YORK

Copyright © Kingfisher 2013
Published in the United States by Kingfisher,
175 Fifth Ave., New York, NY 10010
Kingfisher is an imprint of Macmillan Children's Books, London.
All rights reserved.

Distributed in the U.S. and Canada by Macmillan,
175 Fifth Ave., New York, NY 10010

Series editor: Thea Feldman
Literacy consultant: Ellie Costa, Bank Street College, New York

Library of Congress Cataloging-in-Publication data has been applied for.

ISBN: 978-0-7534-6961-3 (HB)
ISBN: 978-0-7534-6929-3 (PB)

Kingfisher books are available for special promotions
and premiums. For details contact: Special Markets Department,
Macmillan, 175 Fifth Ave., New York, NY 10010.

For more information, please visit www.kingfisherbooks.com

Printed in China
9 8 7 6 5 4 3 2 1
1TR/1012/WKT/UG/105MA

Picture credits
The Publisher would like to thank the following for permission to reproduce their
material. Every care has been taken to trace copyright holders. However, if there
have been unintentional omissions or failure to trace copyright holders, we
apologize and will, if informed, endeavor to make corrections in any future edition.
Top = t; Bottom = b; Center = c; Left = l; Right = r
Cover Shutterstock/Ben Smith, Pages 4 Shutterstock/Zoran Karapancev; 5 Shutterstock/
Ben Jeayes; 6–7 Kingfisher Artbank; 8 Shutterstock/qingqing; 9 Shutterstock/Max Earey; 10
Shutterstock/Ahmad Faizal Yahya; 11 Shutterstock/Walter G. Arce; 12 Shutterstock/Alexander
Kosarev; 13 Getty/Daniel Garcia/AFP; 14–15 Kingfisher Artbank; 14b Getty/John Chapple;
16 Shutterstock/Peter Weber; 17 Shutterstock/Christopher Halloran; 18 Kingfisher Artbank;
19 Shutterstock/Pics-xl; 20 Shutterstock/Andrey Armyagov; 21t Shutterstock/Katherine Welles;
21b Getty/NiklasHalle'n/Barcroft Media; 22 Shutterstock/sonya etchison; 23 Corbis/Tim Wright;
24 Shutterstock/Dmitry Vereshchagin; 25 Corbis/Michael Rosenfeld; 26 Corbis/Steven Vidler
Eurasia Press; 27 Shutterstock/Faiz Zaki; 28 Getty/Grey Wood/AFP; 29 Getty/ChinaFotoPress

Contents

Let's go for a drive!

Every day millions of people around the world ride in cars. They go to work and to school. They go to the doctor, to the library, and many more places. People drive to the local supermarket. Sometimes they drive across the country. Cars make all kinds of trips possible. Where do you like to go in a car?

A shiny new car

Car fact
Today there are more than a thousand million cars in the world.

There are many different kinds of cars. Fasten your seat belt and let's take a look at some!

The first cars

How did people travel before cars? Some people rode horses. Other people traveled in **vehicles**, such as carriages, that were pulled by horses. In the late 1700s, cars with **engines** were invented. An engine is a machine. It makes the car move.

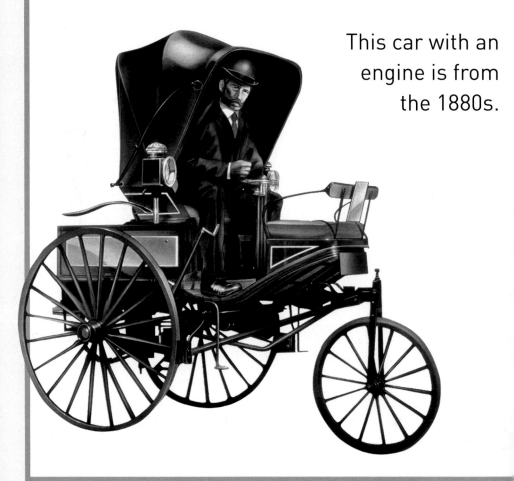

This car with an engine is from the 1880s.

In the 1880s, a man named Karl Benz made the first car with an engine that used **gasoline**. Cars have changed a lot since then. But most of them still use gasoline.

Car fact
Until 1894 cars did not have steering wheels. Drivers used levers to steer and turn a car.

A popular car from the early 1900s

Sports cars

Early cars went less than 10 miles (16 kilometers) an hour. Today, some cars can go over 100 miles (160 kilometers) an hour. Sports cars are one kind of fast car. They have strong engines and wide tires. The tires grip the road. This helps the cars make high-speed turns.

A rounded shape helps with speed.

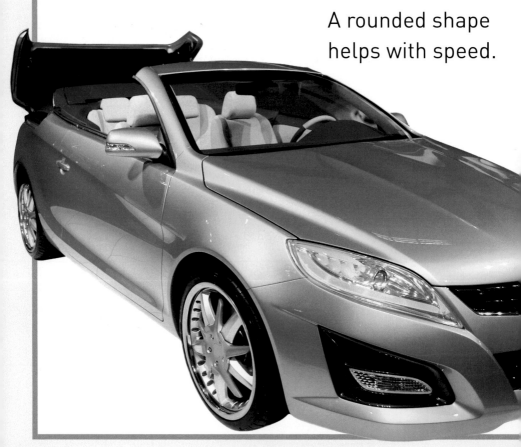

Car fact
A supercar can go as fast as a
speeding train! It can go more than
186 miles (300 kilometers) an hour.

Supercars are the fastest sports cars.
A supercar weighs less than other
sports cars. It has a stronger engine
too. These things help a supercar go
superfast! (For the fastest car of all
time, see page 14.)

Racecars

When does a car need to go really fast? When it's in a race! Sports cars and supercars are often used in races. There are many kinds of racecars. The Formula 1 car is built especially to **compete** at high speeds around a **racetrack**. It has no roof and only room for a driver.

A driver needs a lot of skill to drive so fast! To stay safe, he or she wears a helmet and fireproof suit.

Car fact
During a race, each car has a team at the side of the track. They are ready to quickly change tires or fix car problems.

This team hurries to change all four tires on a car during a race!

Rally cars

Sometimes a race takes place out on the open road. This is called a **rally race**. Cars in a rally race are built to be sturdy. They also have very strong tires.

A rally car can race along muddy roads and dirt paths. It can speed through snow or over a frozen lake! Sometimes a rally car travels at night.

A rally race can be thousands of miles long. And it can take weeks to complete!

Car fact
The Dakar Rally is one of the longest rally races. It takes two weeks. Cars race up to 560 miles (900 kilometers) a day.

Some rally cars race across deserts. They speed over miles of soft sand.

13

World's fastest car

Which car holds the world land speed record? A car called *ThrustSSC*. It reached 763 miles (1,228 kilometers) an hour. That is almost 13 miles (340 meters) a second. It is a little faster than the speed of sound!

"SSC" means **supersonic** car. "Supersonic" means "faster than the speed of sound."

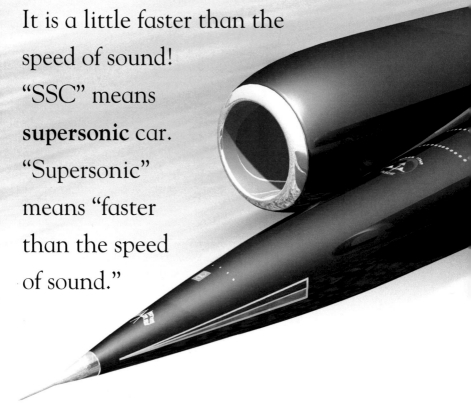

ThrustSSC zooming across the desert.

Car fact
ThrustSSC goes faster than some airplanes fly.

ThrustSSC is 54 feet (16.5 meters) long and 12 feet (3.7 meters) wide. It is at least twice as big as most cars. It has two huge engines. You can see inside one in the above drawing. These are the same kinds of engines used in some fighter planes!

Dragsters

Dragsters come in many shapes and colors. A dragster is a car that can **accelerate** quickly. That means it can go from standing still to racing at high speeds in a few seconds. Its engine helps it do that.

Dragsters compete in **drag races**. A drag race is one quarter of a mile (400 meters) long. It is over in seconds.

These dragsters are ready to race.

At the start of the drag race, drivers spin their wheels. This heats the tires and helps them stay on the road. Then the cars are off. *Zoom!*

Car fact
A parachute helps a dragster slow down at the end of a race.

Start your engine!

Most engines start with a key. The driver puts the key in a lock near the steering wheel. When the key is turned, the engine goes on. Gasoline and air mix together. They get hot enough to burn. That makes the engine work. The car is ready to move!

Car fact
All the moving parts of an engine are covered in oil. The oil helps the parts move smoothly.

The engine makes the car's wheels turn. The wheels move up and down when the car goes over bumps. Each wheel has a rubber tire filled with air. The rubber grips the road and helps the car move smoothly.

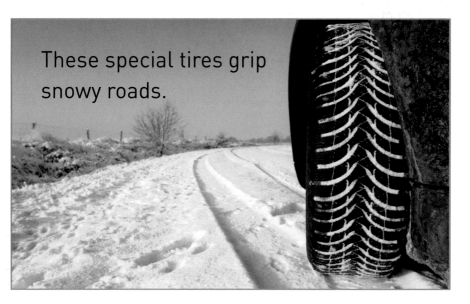

These special tires grip snowy roads.

Learning to drive

Learning to drive takes practice. You practice pressing pedals with your right foot. One pedal makes the car move and speed up. When you lift your foot a little, the car starts to slow down. You press another pedal called the brake to stop the car.

You also learn how to steer the car and make it turn to the left or right.

Car fact
In some countries cars drive on the left side of the road. In most countries they drive on the right side of the road.

When you learn to drive you learn what the road signs mean. You learn many more things too, such as which driver goes first at a crossroads. Before you can drive on your own, you need to pass a driving test. If you do, you get your license!

In some countries the driver's seat is on the right.

Keeping you safe

Everyone tries to drive safely. But sometimes accidents still happen. Cars are built with things, such as seat belts and **airbags**, to help keep you safe. In case of an accident, an airbag in the front of the car opens. It blows up like a balloon and acts like a soft cushion.

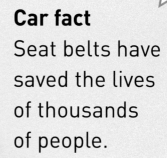

Car fact
Seat belts have saved the lives of thousands of people.

A seat belt goes across your chest and lap.

A car, with a dummy inside,
is being tested for safety.

Researchers test cars to see what happens
in an accident. In a safe work place called
a laboratory, they crash cars. They crash
them into walls or other cars. A **crash-test
dummy** is in the car. The dummy shows the
effect of a crash on a person.

At the car factory

New cars are made all the time. At a factory, machines take sheets of metal. They fold them and join them together. The sheets become the body of a new car.

The body moves through the factory. It is painted. The engine, the doors, and all the other parts are added. Most cars have more than 1,000 parts! Each finished car is tested to make sure it was put together the right way.

People work hard to build a car. Some factories use robots too! Sometimes people and robots work side by side.

Car fact
More than 50 million new cars are built each year. That is one and a half cars a second!

Electric and hybrid cars

Some cars do not have engines. They have **electric motors**. They are electric cars! This kind of car does not use gasoline. It uses a big battery to run the motor. Like any battery, a car battery runs low when used. Then the driver has to find a place to stop. It is time to plug in the battery and recharge it.

Some cars have an engine *and* an electric motor. They are called hybrid cars. The engine starts another machine in the car. That machine starts the motor. It can recharge the battery too. A hybrid car uses less gas than a car with just an engine.

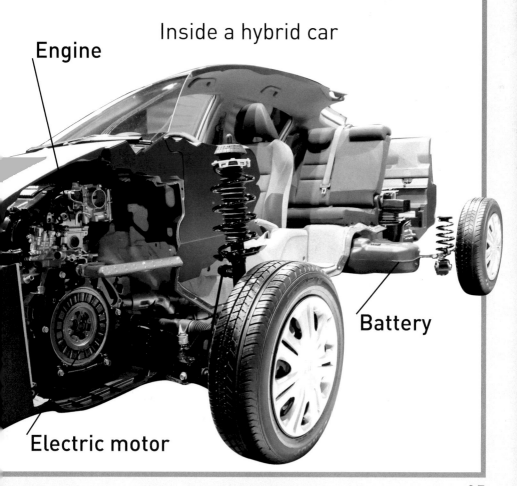

Inside a hybrid car

Engine

Electric motor

Battery

Cars and our planet

Why would you want an electric car? Or a hybrid car? They are good for our planet. They send less **pollution** into the air than cars that run only on gas.

Gas is made from **natural resources**. That means there is only so much of it. We could run out of gas someday if we do not use it carefully. So, it is good to have other ways to make cars run. Scientists are working on more ways for us to use less gas.

Your family can help too. Ride a bike or take a walk!

People in China enjoy a car-free day.

Someday you might be able to have a car like this. It runs on energy from the sun!

Glossary

accelerate to move faster very quickly

airbags parts of a car that help keep people safe in an accident; an airbag will blow up like a ballooon to be a soft thing for people to fall onto

compete to try to win something such as a race

crash-test dummy a life-size doll used to see what might happen to people in a car accident

drag races short races between cars to see which one can accelerate the quickest

electric motors machines that use electricity to make a car move

engines machines that use gasoline to make a car move

gasoline a liquid that makes most car engines work

natural resources things we use that come from the earth

pollution dirt and waste from machines, such as cars, that can poison the air and environment and make it unsafe

racetrack a place where cars race one another

rally race a car race that takes place in public places

supersonic faster than the speed of sound

vehicles things people ride in to get from one place to another

Index